Economics Acknowledge for All Wider

Adel Rivandi

Ehsan Farahani

In this book, I want to explain the achievement of goals in simple and practical steps, that how you can use the law of attraction to achieve your desires. To do this, all the steps must be done carefully and consider a notebook called the Success Notebook so you can do and write down all the exercises in this notebook.

INTRODUCTION

Today, economic knowledge is very important for the whole society. You can be a financial market investor or a manager or a businessman or a shopkeeper or even a housewife; Economic knowledge helps you to know exactly what your surroundings are and to continue to make decisions. So this book is not for a specific group. For all people. Everyone in society i`s dealing with the economy every day. So the need for economic knowledge is not hidden from anyone. Now this book helps you to learn economic concepts in simple language. The existing book is written very simply and fluently and it is tested not to use specialized terms in economics. So any person with any level of knowledge can easily learn the concepts. The book is mostly written based on macroeconomic concepts and is used as well as formally included. Statistics and graphs are taken from the World Bank website as well as the International Monetary Fund.

What is economy?

Humans, companies, factories and communities have unlimited needs and wants, while their resources are limited. Capital and power are limited as the two main sources. Economics seeks to answer the question of how we can meet our limited needs with the limited resources available; Individuals achieve maximum satisfaction and companies and firms achieve maximum profit and communities move towards their goals.

Micro and macro economics

If we examine economic activities at the level of individuals, factories and companies, we have in fact studied microeconomics. On the contrary, if we examine the economic activities of the society and the country, we have in fact studied the macroeconomics.

Alphabet of Economics; Supply and Demand

Undoubtedly, the first and most important lesson to be learned from economies is the concept of supply and demand. Demand in simple terms means at a certain price, how much goods I am willing and able to buy. For example, at the price of $ 5, I buy a loaf of bread. This is where the concept of demand comes into play. The important thing is that the person must be willing and then have the financial ability to buy that product. We must have enough money.

Now what affects demand?

The first and perhaps most important factor is the price of goods. As the price of a commodity increases, so does the demand decrease.

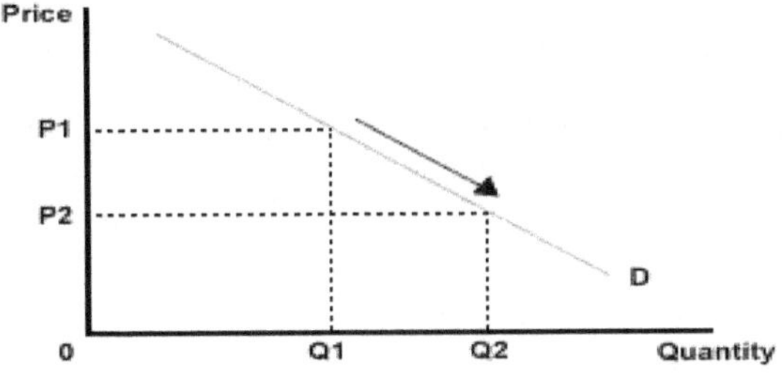

In the figure above, we see the demand curve, which has a downward trend. That is, the relationship between the amount of demand and price is a negative.

The next factor that affects demand is people's income. As people's incomes increase, so does demand.

The next factor that causes the change in demand, the price of substitute goods. Suppose we consume coffee. Now if the price of tea (which replaces coffee) goes down, we want more tea which has become cheaper or suppose if the price of soft drink rises, we go to the consumption of beer. That is, the substitute product of soft drink. Of course, we assumed that our tastes for consumption were the same.

The second letter of the alphabet of economics is supply. Supply or production means how much the producer tends to produce or sell at certain or specific prices.

Suppose you are a clothing manufacturer. Now, for example, due to illegal imports or even smuggling, the price of clothes decreases, it is natural that you have less desire to produce. So the relationship between the amount of production or supply and price is a direct relationship. The higher the price, the more we like to produce.

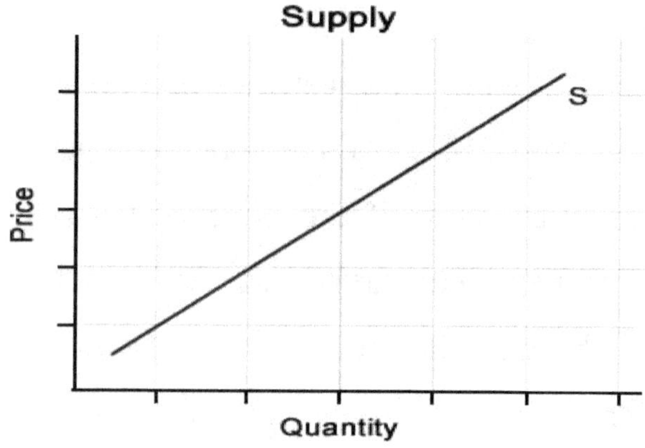

The figure above is the supply curve. We see that the higher the price, the higher the production.

Another factor that affects supply is the cost of production. Like taxes. If the government raises taxes, it is natural for the producer to face higher costs and reduce production.

Elasticity

We use the concept of elasticity to find the sensitivity of one factor to changes in another.

Demand elasticity

Types of demand elasticity:

1: Price elasticity of demand: show the responsiveness, or elasticity or sensitive, of the quantity demanded of a good or service to a change in its price.

High sensitivity. For example, if the price of a commodity increases, demand will fall sharply. For example, if the price of a luxury car increases, the demand for it will decrease by a greater amount.

Low sensitivity. For example, if the price of a good increases, demand will fall lower and demand does not change many.

2: Cross-price elasticity of demand: show the responsiveness, or elasticity or sensitive, of the quantity demanded of a good or service to changes in the price of a different product.

For example, Pepsi Co raises the price of its soft drinks. What changes does this make to the demand for Coca-Cola soft drinks?

3: Income elasticity of demand: Income elasticity of demand is a measure used to show the responsiveness of the quantity demanded of a good or service to a change in the consumer income.

For example, your income should increase by 5%. How does this change the amount of your demand?

Elasticity of supply

Price elasticity of supply

Shows how many production and supply change if the price of goods changes.

Gross Domestic Product (GDP)

We may have heard the word many times in economic analysis and news. GDP is important because it is used as the most important indicator of economic performance of governments in economic analysis.

GDP means the total final products and services produced in a country over a period of time (for example, one year) by the people living in that country. The nationality of the person is not important here. It is only important that they live in a certain geographical area.

GDP is calculated either at the current market price or at the base price. So what difference do they make?

Suppose, for example, that only two products of

bread and rice are produced in a country's economy; In 2010, for example, we produced 3 kilos of rice worth $ 5 per kilo and 10 loaves of bread worth $ 1 per unit. Well, what is the value of our GDP in 2010?

The dollar value of rice is 5 * 3 = 15 and bread is 1 * 10 = 10, so the sum of the two becomes $ 25. That is the total gross domestic product at market prices in that year.

Next year (2011) we produce 4 kilos of rice worth $ 7 per kilo and 12 loaves of bread worth $ 2 per unit. Our total GDP at market prices this year will be $ 52.

Here we calculate GDP at current value or market price. Because we used this year's prices.

So what if we want to calculate 2011 GDP at base value (base price)? Well, here we measure the amount of production in terms of 2011, but the prices in terms of a specific year, for example here in 2010. 2010 will be the base year.

Well, in 2011, we produced 6 kilos of rice worth

$ 5 per unit (base year price) and 12 loaves of bread worth $ 1 per unit (base year price). Gross domestic product (GDP) in 2011 will be at a base price (2010) of $ 42.

So why is base value important to us? Well, of course, we have eliminated the effect of rising prices here and only focused on increasing or decreasing the amount of production.

The GDP at market price called nominal GDP.

Real Gross Domestic Product

Real GDP is a macroeconomic statistic that measures the value of the goods and services produced by an economy in a specific period, adjusted the inflation (changes in price). It means that Real GDP eliminates the effect of price changes.

Year	Nominal GDP (trillions)	Real GDP (trillions)
2013	$16.785	$16.495
2014	$17.527	$16.912
2015	$18.238	$17.432
2016	$18.745	$17.731
2017	$19.543	$18.144
2018	$20.612	$18.688
2019	$21.433	$19..092

The above chart shows both nominal and real GDP.

Economic Growth

Well, as we said, the concept of GDP value is one of the key parts of measuring government performance. Because the measure of economic growth is how much our production has gone up or down.

Economic growth means the growth or decrease of GDP compared to the previous period.

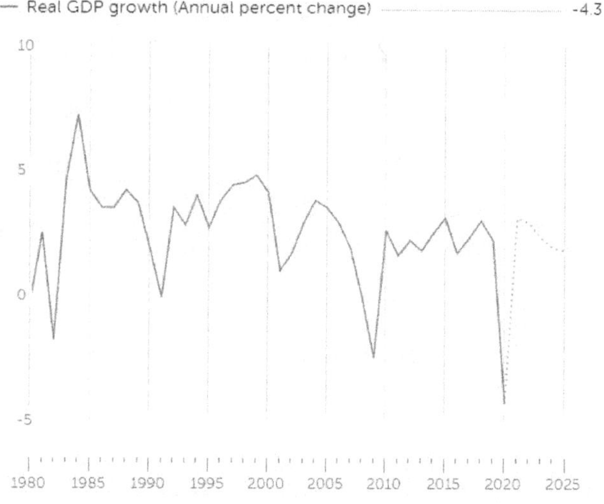

In 1981, President Reagan cut taxes and the

recession ended in 1982 and resulted in the 1983 and 1984 America's economic growth rate is rising.

The above chart is economic growth rate in USA. In 2007 and 2008, the US economic growth rate slowed due to the financial crisis.

In early 2020, the widespread outbreak of the coronavirus caused the US economic growth rate to plummet.

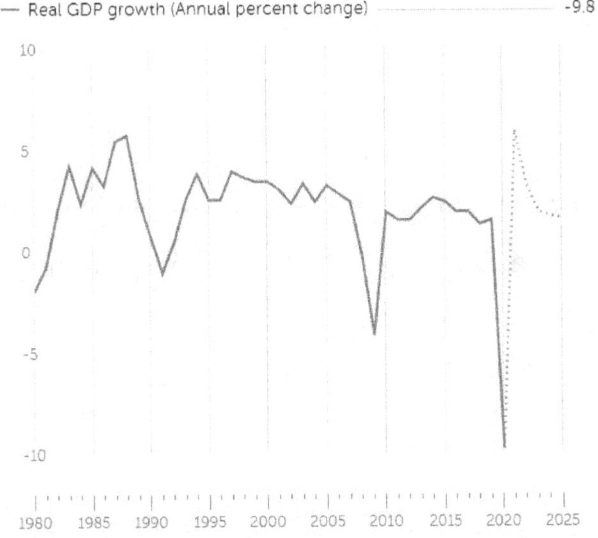

The chart above shows the UK economic growth rate. The historic fall in the country's economic

growth rate in early 2020 was due to the outbreak
of the Corona virus

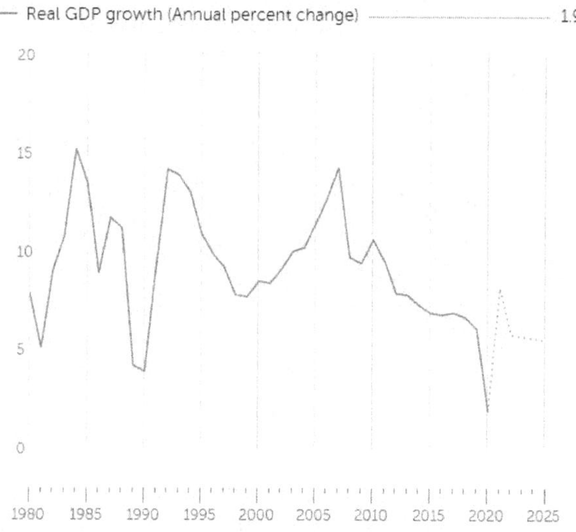

The chart above shows China's economic growth
rate. China was less affected by the Corona virus
than UK.

Gross National Income (GNI)

GNI is the total amount of money earned by a nation's people and businesses.

Gross national income is an indicator for measuring the wealth of individuals in society.

Net national income (NNI)

NNI is gross national income minus the depreciation of fixed capital assets.

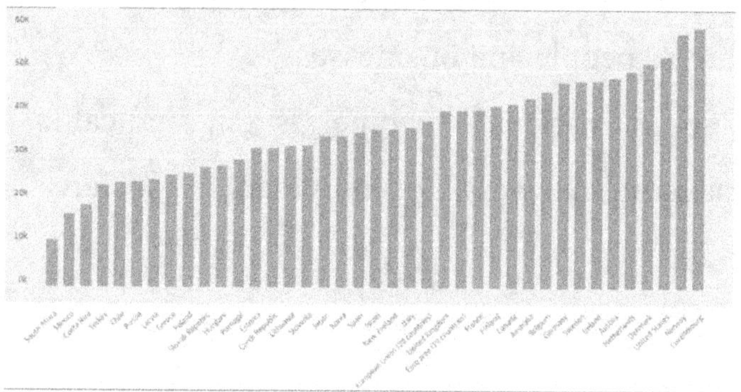

The chart above shows the net national income of countries in 2018. As you can see, Luxembourg has a higher net national income.

Per capita income

Per capita income is a measure of the amount of money earned per person in a nation or geographic region.

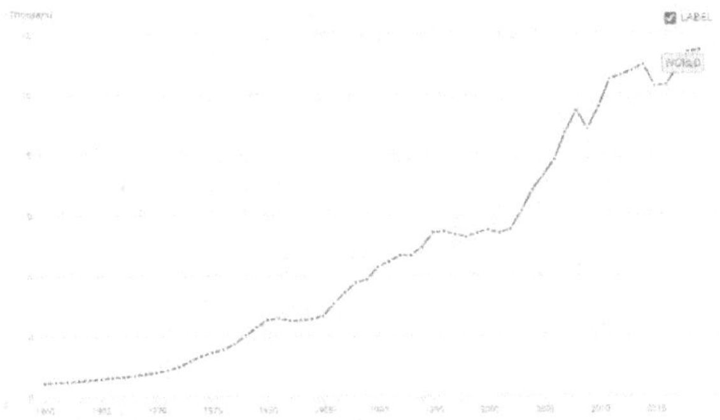

The chart above shows Per capita income from 1960 to 2019. As you can see, this is an uptrend. This means that the world has become richer.

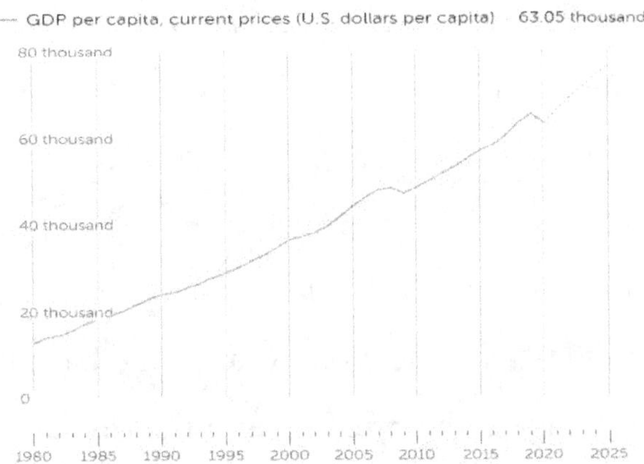

This is GDP per capita for USA

Price index

In the previous article, we discussed total production in economics. Another important quantity in economics is the issue of prices. In other words, for economic analysis, it is necessary to create a quantity on the basis of which we can judge and comment on all prices in the form of a summary number. We need to create a criterion that expresses the general situation of prices or all prices in the form of a number.

Price indices are used to examine the trend of price changes over time. By comparing price indices over time, one can judge how prices change over time.

The price index is a kind of average price. For the price index, we select one year as the base year and then compare the price index in one year with it.

A price index can be a consumer or producer price index. The consumer price index indicates the change in the price of goods and services consumed by households. Based on the price index, we can examine how the pressure on consumers due to changes in the prices of goods and services during these years.

Producer price index also means the trend of changing commodity prices for producers.

year	CPI
2010	100
2011	106.9
2012	112.4
2013	119.4
2014	126.9
2015	138.4
2016	150.5
2017	155.7
2018	161.4
2019	167.4

The table above shows the consumer price index in Brazil. We consider one year as the base year (here 2010) and then set the index number in the base year to 100. Now we compare the index number in different years with 100. For example, the index in 2014 was equal to 126.9. This average price for Brazilian consumers in 2014 increased by 26.9% compared to 2010. Another example in 2018 is the index equal to 161.4. This means that the average price of goods and services in 2018 compared to 2010, increased by 61.4%. By examining the indicators, we can understand the growing trend of prices in different years.

year	CPI
2010	100
2011	126.3
2012	160.7
2013	219.5
2014	256
2015	288
2016	308
2017	333.7
2018	393.8
2019	550.9

The chart above shows the consumer price index in Iran. As you can see, this index has had a very upward trend. For example, this index reached 308 in 2016, which indicates that prices in Iran in 2016 compared to 2010, 2.08 times. Divide the number 308 by 100 and then subtract 1. Now this number has reached 550.9 in 2019. In other words, prices have increased 4.5 times compared to 2010.

PPI

Producer price index refers to the average growth rate of prices for producers.

year	PPI
2015	100
2016	91.9
2017	87.7
2018	93.7

The table above shows the value of the producer price index in Iceland. The base year is 2015 in which the index is equal to 100. As you can see, for example, in 2018, when the index is below 100, that is, production costs in Iceland have decreased compared to 2015.

Year	PPI
2015	100
2016	105.6
2017	124.1
2018	157.1

The table above shows the value of the producer price index in Turkey.

Inflation

Inflation means the rate of change in average prices. The concept of price change rate or inflation rate is used to determine the intensity of price changes in a particular year.

Inflation is the decline of purchasing power of a given currency over time and falling the currency of that country.

In inflation, we measure the average price of goods compared to the previous year

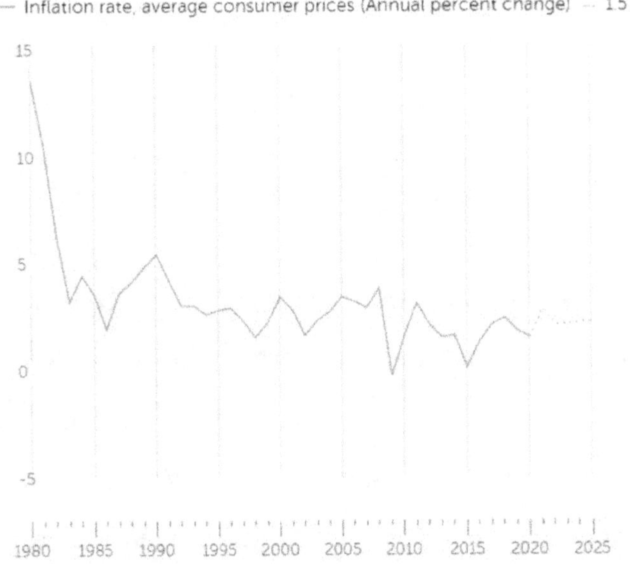

This is the inflation rate of the USA. The US

inflation rate is now 1.5 percent. This means that goods and services in the United States have increased by 1.5 percent this year compared to last year.

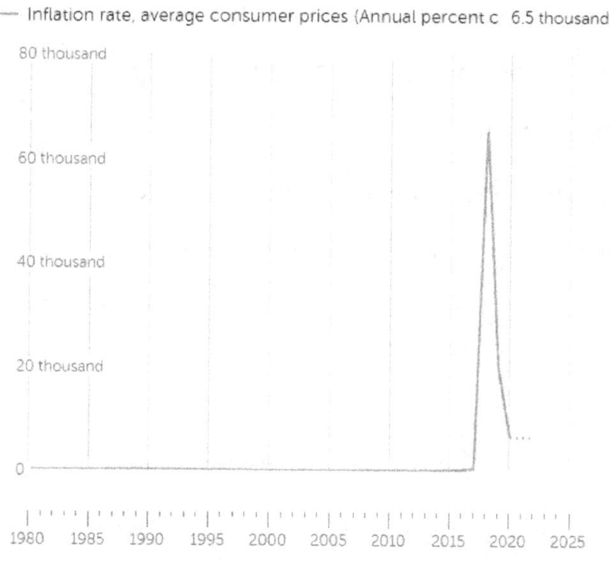

This is inflation rate of Venezuela. The inflation reached to 65 thousand percent in 2018. Now the inflation rate is 6.5 thousand percent. This means that goods and services in Venezuela have increased by 6.5 thousand percent this year compared to last year.

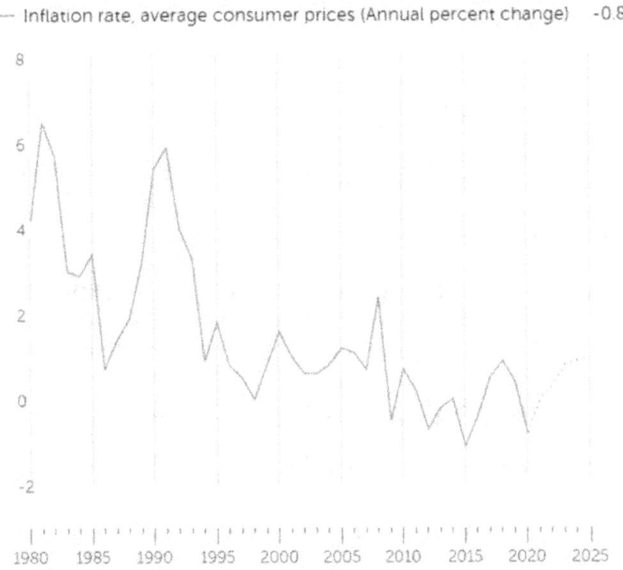

Switzerland's inflation has reached negative 0.8 percent in 2020. This means that this year's goods are cheaper than last year.

Causes of inflation

Inflation is generally caused in the economy for 3 reasons:

1 Increase in production costs: Whenever the raw materials of goods become more expensive, as a result, the goods will cost more for the producer, and as a result, he will have to sell those goods more expensively. Labor may become more expensive.

2 Increase money supply. If money and liquidity increase in the economy and production does not grow as a result, that excess money will cause inflation.

3 Inequality of supply and demand: When demand is higher than supply, inflation occurs.

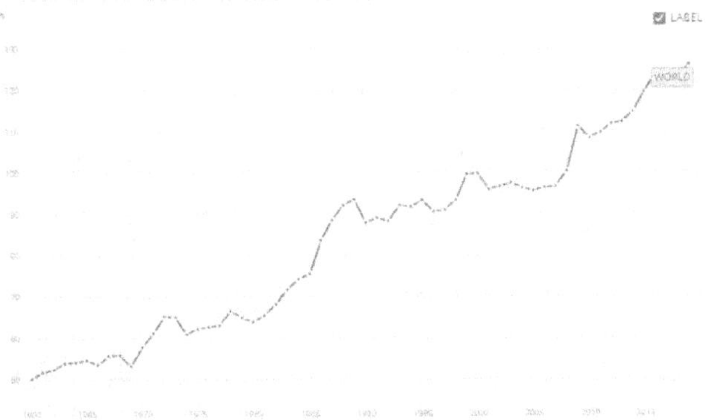

You see the ratio of liquidity to GDP in the world. Its growing trend shows an increase in liquidity relative to production. This can cause global inflation.

This chart shows the liquidity to GDP of USA.

Recession

A recession is a situation in which the economic activities of a society fall sharply for more than a few months. For example, goods are not sold. There is no effective demand in the market. Supply is more than demand. The decline in GDP is generally a sign of a recession. That is, economic growth is negative. The recession is generally accompanied by inflation.

Stagflation

There may be periods of recession and inflation in the economy together, which is called stagflation. For example, suppose the price of a house has gone up, and this means that inflation and the growth of the price of a house have caused a lack of effective and good demand for purchase, and this means a recession. This is where the stagflation occurred.

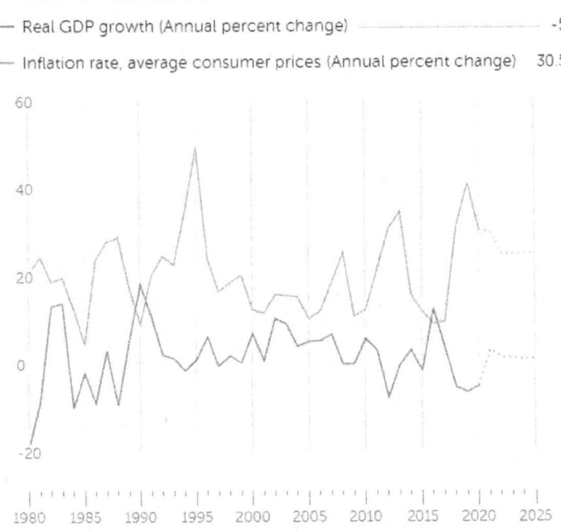

This is a chart of economic growth as well as inflation in Iran. As you can see, since almost 2016, we have been facing an increase in inflation (blue chart) and Iran's economic growth rate (red) has been declining since 2016 and has even reached negative. This could be a sign of a stagflation in the economy.

Money

In the simplest definition, money is what is traded and accepted by everyone.

Uses of money

1 Exchange: Any person can receive money in exchange for selling their goods or services.

2 Measurement or counting device: Money is used to show, measure and compare the value and price of goods.

3 Value storage device: A person can set aside his wealth for the future in the form of money. If a person keeps his savings in the form of cash (in today's world of banknotes and bank deposits), we say that money is a reserve of value.

All kinds of money

1 Commodity money: In different societies, commodity money included various forms such as salt, spices, precious stones, animal skins, and so on. Commodity money that is actually used in the exchange and trade of goods for goods. But these had problems with the exchange. For example, some were not portable; They were either perishable or could not be broken down into smaller parts. For this reason, human beings began to create commodity money in the form of precious metals, gold and silver, and the rest of commodity money, such as salt and animal skins, became obsolete. Because gold and silver as commodity money, they were easy to transport, incorruptible and could be broken into smaller components and were able to spread as commodity money in societies.

2 Paper money or banknotes: People who had

gold or silver and did not need it for a while, lent it to a money changer and received a gold or silver receipt in return. The money changer promised to return their gold and silver to the depositor upon receive of the gold or silver receipt. The money changers soon realized that part of the gold and silver that remained with them was, in other words, useless. In order to be able to use the gold and silver they do not have at their disposal, the holders of gold and silver receipts were allowed to buy gold and silver instead of going to the money changer instead of going to the money changer. Deliver the same receipt to the seller of the goods, and if the seller of the goods wishes, they can go to the money changer to get the gold and silver using those receipts. Ever since the use of these receipts became commonplace in trade, these receipts have become the means of exchange and therefore money, and thus paper money was invented.

3 Bank Deposit or Cheque: After money changers created paper money, the government

transferred the monopoly of issuing banknotes to a bank called the Central Bank, depriving other banks and money changers of the possibility of issuing banknotes. Although other banks lost the ability to issue banknotes, they were able to provide other banking services such as deposits or lending. In fact, commercial banks were able to issue banknotes issued by the central bank to individuals. Take a deposit and rely on it, in addition to keeping the depositor money, to create money by lending. Now the bank, which had taken the person's money, was opening a demand account for him. The depositor can withdraw money from his account at any time. That is, if a person deposited $ 100 in a bank, the bank owed him $ 100, and he could withdraw it whenever he wanted. For withdrawal from the account, a batch of cheque was delivered to the customer. In this way, a person's money was in the form of bank money or office money instead of paper money or banknotes. This means that whenever a person needed money, he could withdraw money from his bank account by cheque.

4 It is now possible to use current deposits in buying and selling using a debit card or using an ID and password online. Like the same online purchases that are made in the context of a payment gateway.

Money Supply (M1)

The amount of money in banknotes and coins in the hands of the people plus demand deposits. The sum of these two are money.

Liquidity (M2)

Liquidity is a comprehensive definition of money. Liquidity is the sum of money (same as banknotes, coins, and demand deposits) and cash equivalent. Cash equivalent refers to savings deposits and time deposit. For this reason, they are called quasi-money, because they are quickly converted into cash and used for trade when needed.

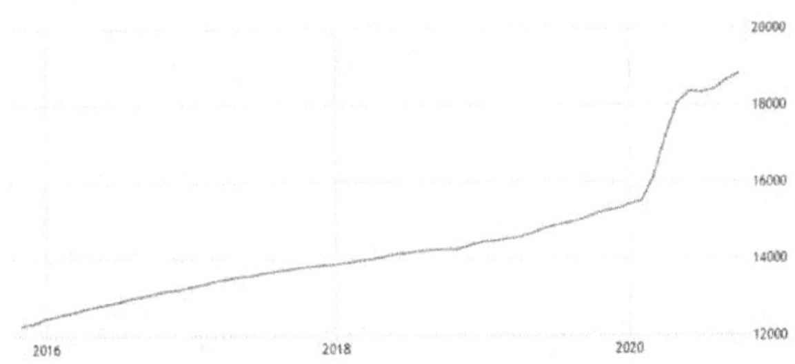

The chart above also shows liquidity in the

United States. With the creation of the Corona virus, the US Federal Reserve has begun printing large amounts of money and liquidity has risen in the country.

When liquidity rises, it causes inflation and also devalues the national currency.

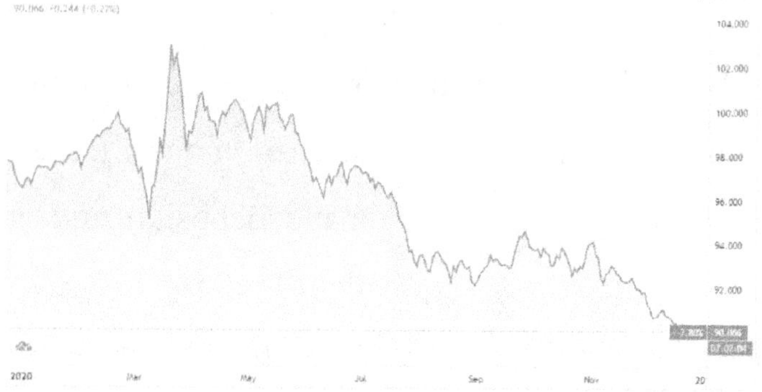

You see the trend of the US Dollar Index. One of the factors that devalued the dollar was the printing of money.

Monetary Base

The monetary base refers to the amount of cash circulating in the economy. These are Including of currency and reversal banks. Currency refers to banknotes and coins held by people. Bank reserves are cash deposits in the commercial banks. In a simple definition, the monetary base is the currency generated by the central bank. The monetary base is a component of a nation's money supply.

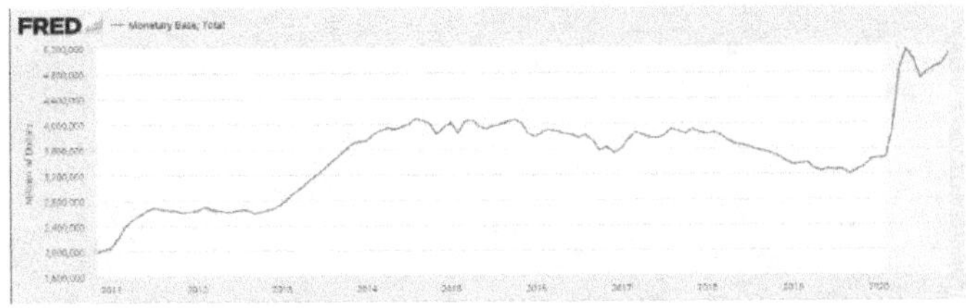

The chart above shows the trend of the monetary base in the United States. The growth of the monetary base increase liquidity in the economy.

The above definitions indicate that only part of

the money is created by the central bank and not all of it. The central bank only creates money if it has an asset to back it up.

Money multiplier

The money multiplier indicates how much of a dollar will be created in the economy if a dollar is created by the central bank.

For example, if the multiplier of money is 3, that is, for every $ 1 of money created by the central bank (increase in the monetary base), eventually $ 3 of new liquidity will be created.

$ 1 out of $ 3 is created by the central bank (raising the monetary base) and the other $ 2 is created by the commercial banks. Commercial banks create liquidity by attracting people's deposits and lending from deposits.

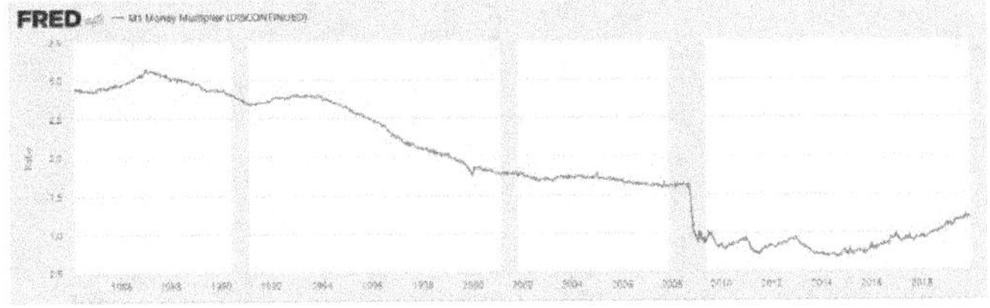

The chart above shows the trend of the money multiplier in the USA.

Federal Reserve

The Federal Reserve System is the central banking system of the United States of America.

Purpose of Federal Reserve

To manage the nation's money supply through monetary policy

To supervise and regulate banking institutions

Stable prices, including prevention of either inflation or deflation

To provide financial services to depository institutions, the U.S. government, and foreign official institutions

To facilitate the exchange of payments among regions.

The Federal Reserve Balance sheet

It lists all assets and liabilities, providing a consolidated statement of the condition of all 12 regional Federal Reserve Banks. The Fed's assets consist primarily of government securities and the loans it extends to its regional banks. Its liabilities include U.S. currency in circulation.

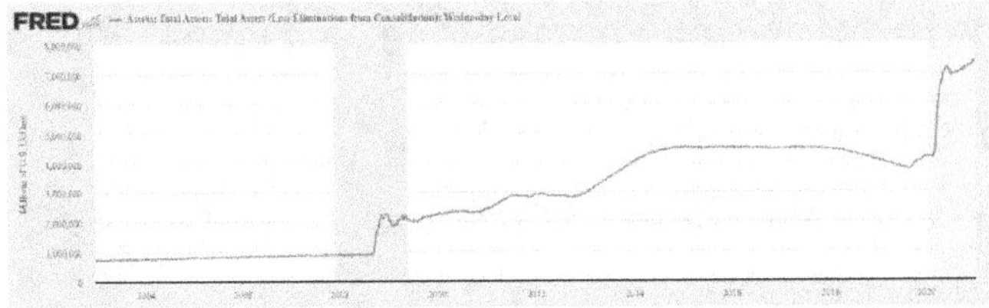

Increase the balance sheet of the US Federal Reserve from 2020. Increasing the balance sheet of the US Federal Reserve will increase liquidity.

Demand for money

Asking for money means keeping money, not spending it. For example, if a person has $ 100 in his pocket and $ 400 in his current account, he demands for a total of $ 500.

Now, for what reasons does a person keep money?

1 Exchange and transaction: a person wants to buy goods later and provide for his necessities. So he keeps the money so that he can buy the goods he needs later.

2 A precautionary reason, as an unexpected need can often arise

3 Speculation: Sometimes we know that in the future a market like the stock market or gold will be attractive for investment. Now we keep the money to invest in those markets in the future.

Monetary policy

Monetary policies are policies that change liquidity in society.

Types of monetary policies

Expansionary Monetary Policy

This is a monetary policy that aims to increase the money supply in the economy. When the economy is in a state of recession, this kind of policy and the increase of money in the society will create economic prosperity.

Contractionary Monetary Policy

The goal of a contractionary monetary policy is to decrease the money supply in the economy. When the economy is in a state of inflation and the amount of money in the society is high, by implementing these types of policies, they control the liquidity and collect money from the society.

So how can the central bank change liquidity in the economy?

1 Open market operations:

The central bank can either purchase or sell securities issued by the government to affect the money supply. When the central bank wants to pursue expansionary monetary policy through open market operations, it buys government bonds. Because when it buys, it gives money to people and buys from them, and this causes the amount of money to increase.

2 Interest rate adjustment:

A central bank can influence interest rates by changing the discount rate. The discount rate is an interest rate charged by a central bank to banks for short-term loans. For example, if a central bank increases the discount rate, the cost of borrowing for the banks increases. Subsequently, the banks will increase the interest rate they charge their customers. Thus, the cost of borrowing in the economy will increase, and the money supply will decrease.

3 Change reserve requirements:

Central banks usually set up the minimum amount of reserves that must be held by a commercial bank.

If monetary policies increase the required reserve amount, commercial banks find less money available to lend to their clients and thus, money supply decreases.

Fiscal policy

Fiscal policy is a set of government actions that change the demand in the economy.

Types of fiscal policies

There are generally two types of fiscal policy:

1 Expansionary fiscal policy: This type of policy increases demand. When society is in recession, with the implementation of this type of policy, demand grows.

2 Contraceptive fiscal policy: This type of policy reduces demand. Whenever there is high inflation in society (demand is higher than supply), demand can be controlled by implementing this type of policy.

So how can the government implement its fiscal policies?

1 Change in taxes: Whenever the government reduces taxes, it pursues an expansionary fiscal policy. Because when the government reduces taxes, there is more money left for people and it

increases their purchasing power. (Demand increases)

Well, whenever the government raises taxes, it reduces people's purchasing power and reduces demand, and this is a contractionary fiscal policy.

2 Changes in government spending: Increasing government spending is an expansionary fiscal policy. When society is in a recession, the government helps increase demand by increasing its spending (for example, doing more projects). Because the government needs goods and services to carry out its projects. So the demand goes up. Reducing government spending is a contractionary fiscal policy.

Gini coefficient

One of the indicators for measuring inequality in society is the Gini coefficient. The Gini coefficient is a number between zero and one. The closer it is to zero, that is, the more equal wealth and income are distributed in society, and the closer it is to 1, the more unequal the distribution of income and wealth in society is.

Unemployment

From an economic point of view, an unemployed person is someone who is looking for a job but cannot find anything.

The unemployment rate means what percentage of our active population is unemployed. The active population is the sum of the unemployed and employed people.

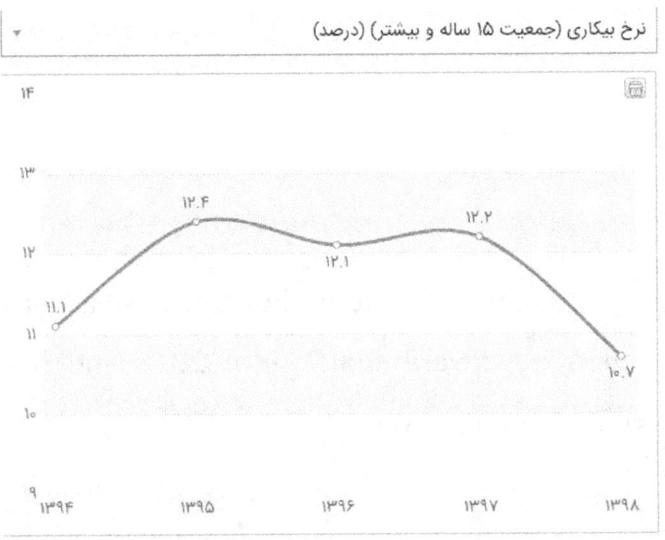

As you can see, Iran's unemployment rate in 2019 has reached 10.7%. This means that out of every 100 people in our active population, 10.7 are unemployed. Meanwhile, in the summer of 2019, the unemployment rate has reached 9.5%.

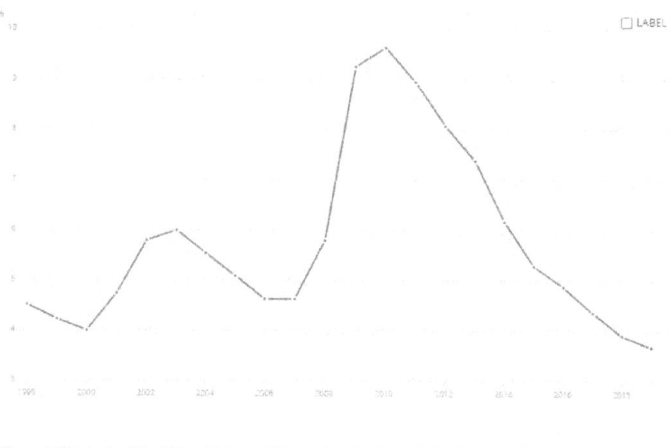

The unemployment rate in the United States has been on a downward trend since 2011 and has reached its lowest point in 2019.

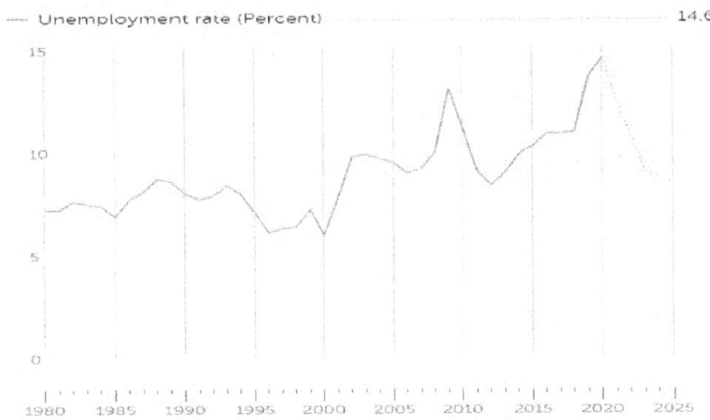

The unemployment rate in Turkey has reached 14.6% in 2020.

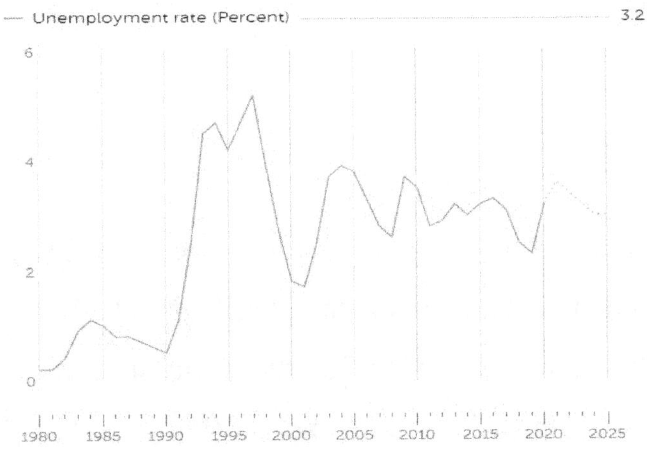

The unemployment rate in Switzerland has reached 3.2% in 2020.

Economic participation rate

It is the total active population (employed and unemployed) to the total population.

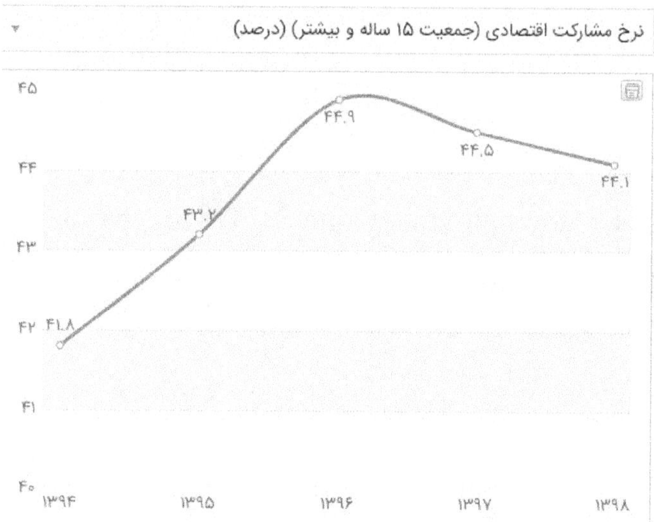

The economic participation rate for 2018 has reached 44.1%. This means that only 41.1% of the total population over 15 years old in Iran were either employed or unemployed (looking for a job) and the rest are not divided into any of these two groups. The low economic participation rate indicates that a significant percentage of the population, at working ages, are not present in the labor market and in fact they are out of the active population of the country.

Money laundering

Money laundering means turning dirty money into clean money. When a person commits a crime (smuggling of goods, drugs, fraud, embezzlement, theft, etc.) and obtains property through it, he is always looking for a way to hide the nature and origin of this illegitimate property; so he launders money. Money laundering is the process in which dirty money (or money obtained through illegal means) is converted into clean money or wealth that is ostensibly obtained through legitimate means so that the original source of the money is unknown.

Rent

Rent is a black word in economics. In a simple definition, rent is an income without direct reliance on labor and productive effort and the risk of economic activity. Rent in the economy is any payment to the owner or agent of the production, over the required costs and related profits. This means that, in addition to the interest that the person has, we pay him or her. Here the rent is formed. In the political literature, when a particular privilege or monopoly is granted to a particular producer that others cannot benefit from, the supply of that product will be limited and as a result of increased demand, prices will rise and economic rents will accrue to that producer.

What is rent-seeking?

In the general definition, rent-seeking is an economic activity by which an individual or economic unit can increase its income without creating more added value.

Rent-seeking occurs when large corporations use economic resources, such as bribery and lobbying to pressure governments to enact new laws such as restricting imports, preventing new companies from entering the market and controlling prices to provide the conditions that these companies want.

Misery index

The sum of the unemployment rate and the inflation rate is called the misery index.

year	2011	2012	2013	2014	2015	2016	2017	2018
Misery index	41.6%	43.2%	25.2%	22.1%	19.3%	20.3%	38.9%	45.5%

We see the misery index in Iran, which has been declining since 1992 but has been rising since 1997.

Balance of payments

Today, with the expansion of international exchanges, whether in the form of goods and services or the form of capital transfers or asset exchanges, issues related to the balance of payments and the foreign exchange market have become extremely important. This is important both for the impact and developments inside and outside an economy on the balance of payments and the foreign exchange market and for the impact of foreign exchange market developments on the domestic economy.

Now what is the balance of payments? Balance of payments is an account in which all transactions of domestic people with foreign people are recorded. If we assume that we show all the transactions of domestic and foreign people in the balance of payments account in the form of a T account, then:

Items are recorded that lead to the receipt of exchange from foreign people	Items are recorded that lead to the payments of exchange to foreign people

The balance of payments account is now divided into two current accounts and a capital account. That is, the current account and capital are components of the balance of payments account.

Current account: It is an account in which all transactions of goods and services are insured by domestic and foreign people, like export and import.

Import

export of goods and services that lead to the payment of exchange	Import of goods and services that lead to the payment of exchange

The right side of this T account is the outflow of

money and exchange from the country. While on the left is the entry of exchange into the country. For example, we import $10 million worth of goods. This is recorded on the right. Because we have money leaving the country. If the right is more than the left (imports exceed exports), it is said that the trade or current account balance has a deficit. Conversely, if the left is more than the right (exports exceed imports), it is said that the trade or current account balance has a surplus.

Capital account

It is an account in which all transactions of assets between foreign and domestic are recorded, such as buying and selling company stocks or land and real estate.

sell assets to foreigners (currency entry)	Buy assets from foreigners(exchange outflow)

On the right is the purchase of assets from foreigners. While on the left, the sale of assets to foreigners is recorded.

The sum of the two current and capital accounts forms the balance of payments account.

Well if the right is more than the left (buying assets is more than selling assets), the capital account balance or net capital inflow is said to be negative. Conversely, if the left is more than the right, we have a positive capital account balance or capital surplus.

Well, as we said, a balance of payments account is created from the sum of these two accounts. So in a nutshell:

The balance of payments account' balance is equal to the sum of the receipts from the foreigners minus the sum of the payments to them.

Well, if the balance is positive, it means that the total receipts were more than the payments and we had exchange entry to the country. So we have a balance of payments surplus. But if the balance is negative, it means that the sum of the foreign payments is more than the receipts and the outflow of exchange has occurred. So we have a balance of payments deficit.

Well, in general, if we have a balance of payments surplus, it means that the inflow of exchange is more than the outflow of it; So we have an oversupply of exchange and this will cause the exchange rate to fall or the national money to increase.

Now, if the balance of payments account has a negative balance, it will cause a shortage of exchange supply or an excess demand for exchange and the exchange rate in that country will increase and the national money will depreciate.

آمارماهانه صادرات و واردات گمرکی کشور(۱)						۲
صادرات (۲)			واردات			سال ۱۳۹۹
ارزش واحد	مقدار(هزارتن)	ارزش (میلیون دلار)	ارزش واحد	مقدار(هزارتن)	ارزش (میلیون دلار)	
۳۰۹	۵۳۴۶	۱۶۵۲	۷۶۴	۲۵۲۶	۱۹۳۱	فروردین
۲۸۹	۹۱۷۶	۲۶۴۸	۸۰۲	۳۸۷۹	۳۱۱۰	اردیبهشت
۲۷۹	۷۴۰۷	۳۰۶۴	۱۰۳۴	۲۵۱۸	۲۵۷۹	خرداد
۲۸۱	۸۳۵۶	۳۳۴۹	۱۱۵۱	۲۸۷۰	۳۳۰۲	تیر
۲۷۸	۷۷۸۱	۳۱۶۲	۱۳۶۵	۲۰۴۱	۲۷۸۵	مرداد
۳۲۶	۸۲۵۲	۳۶۹۱	۱۱۴۳	۲۶۹۰	۳۰۷۶	شهریور
۲۹۳	۴۶۳۱۸	۱۳۵۶۶	۱۰۱۶	۱۶۵۲۴	۱۶۷۸۳	کل دوره

Well, as you can see in the table above, Iran's imports in the first six months of 2019 has reached

16,783 million dollars. While the value of Iran's exports in the first six months of 2019 has reached 13566 million dollars. Well, as we can see, the value of the imports has been higher than the exports, which creates excess demand. If the central bank has some exchanges, it can respond to this demand by distributing it; otherwise, it will increase the exchange rate.

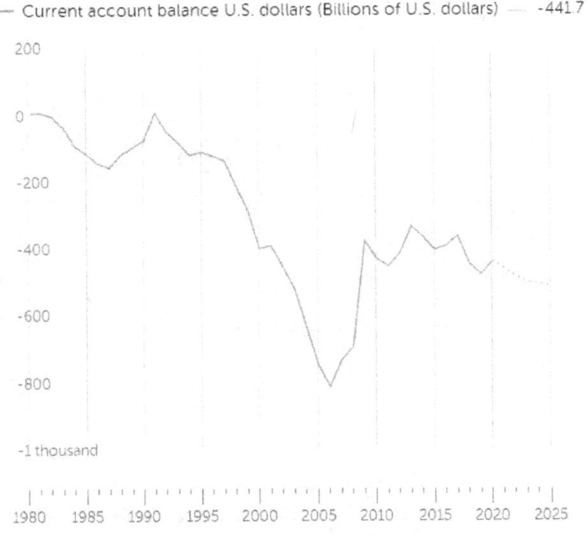

Well, in the figure above, we see the current account of the United States, which in 2019 has a deficit of 480 billion dollars.

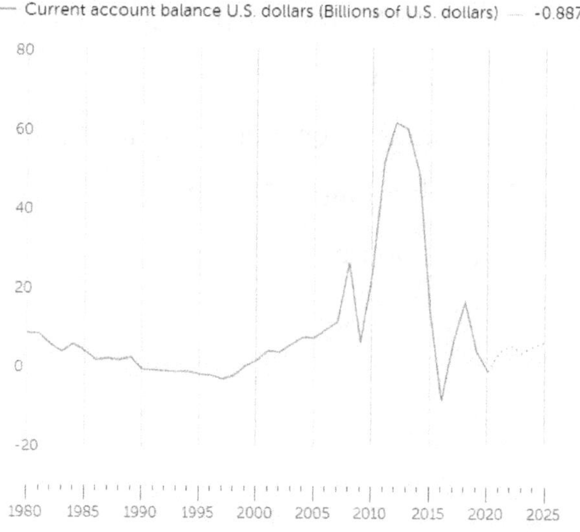

The current account of Qatar in 2020 has reached a deficit of $ 0.8 billion.

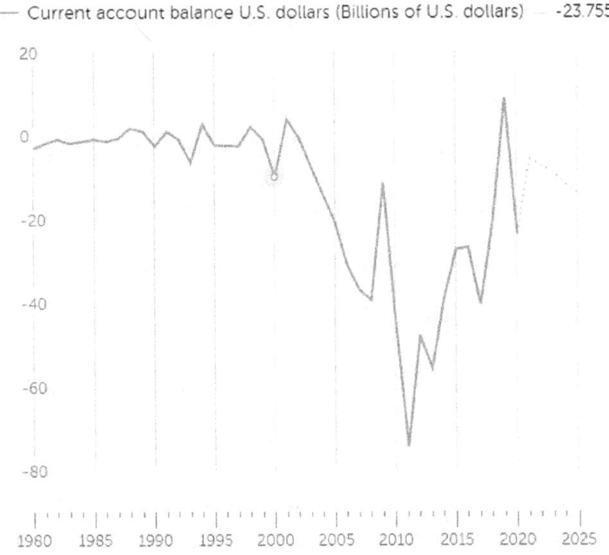

In the chart above, we can see that Turkey's trade balance account has reached $ 23.755 billion.

Interest rate

in a simple definition, an interest rate is the price of money. You have probably borrowed from a bank. The bank will ask you for the interest rate. This is actually the cost you have to pay to get a loan. The main reason for the interest rate in the economy is the time value of money and the opportunity cost. In the economies, money depreciates over time due to the inflation and to compensate for this depreciation, you will be asked for the interest rate. Another reason for the interest rate is the opportunity cost. Those who lend you money deprive themselves of investing in other assets. To compensate for this deprivation, they will ask you for the interest rate. For example, when you put money in the bank and receive interest, it is the same as compensating for the opportunity cost. In the economy, when the inflation rate goes up, so does the interest rate. In the economies facing high inflation, such as Iran, borrowing can be very useful due to the mismatch between the interest rate and inflation. For example, if you took a loan in 2015, you have faced a depreciation in the following years. This means that the installments and interests you pay to the bank have decreased in value in the following years. The payment amount may be fixed, but the value of 1 million dollar in 2016 is not the same as the value of 1 million$ in2018.

year	2013	2014	2015	2016	2017	2018	2019
Bank interest rate	22%	20%	15%	15%	15%	15%	15%

As we can see, since 2016, the bank interest rate is

much lower than the inflation rate. For this reason, we witnessed the outflow of money from the banks and its entry into other markets. This is because the real interest rate was negative. When we say that the bank interest rate in 2019 is 15%, we are referring to the nominal interest rate. Now we have to subtract this rate from the annual inflation rate to reach the real interest rate. Because we have to spend part of our interest on reducing purchasing power (inflation) and what is left is added to our purchasing power.

2018	2017	2016	2015	2014	2013	year
15%	15%	15%	15%	20%	22%	Nominal interest rate
34.8%	26.9%	8.2%	6.9%	11.1%	15.6%	inflation

						rate
-19.8%	-11.9%	6.8%	8.1%	8.9%	6.4%	Real interest rate

In the table above, as we see, for example, in 2013, the real interest rate has reached 6.4%. This is true that you get 22% profit from the bank, but you give 15.6% of it to inflation. Anything left is counted as your main profit. Since 2017, the real interest rate has been negative in Iran. This means that if you put money in the bank and made a profit, you still couldn't cover inflation and even with a profit from the bank, your purchasing power would decrease by 11.9%. Whenever the real interest rate becomes negative in the economy and this trend continues (becomes more negative), people bring their capital to assets that can protect themselves against this devaluation. In this situation, the tendency to the stock market, gold, real estate, and other capital assets   will   increase.

Interest rate	country
38%	Venezuela
15%	Turkey
7%	Pakistan
-0.75%	Switzerland
4%	Iraq
2.5%	Qatar
0.25%	US

In the table above, we see the interest rate of several countries. For example in Switzerland, the interest rate is negative. For example, if you put money in the bank, you have to pay some extra money to keep them for you.

You see the real interest rate of US. The upward trend of real interest rates has started since 2014.

The chart above shows the real interest rate in Canada, which fluctuate in a certain range. Those who intend to immigrate or invest in a country must consider these things. Countries with negative real rates (high inflation rate) are not a good option for immigration.

Oil

Oil is one of the non _renewable fossil fuels used to produce products such as gasoline, naphtha, and jet fuels. Lower density oils are light oils and higher density oils are heavy oils.

Oils that have less sulfur are sweet oil and oils that have more sulfur are sour oil.

Types of crude oil

Brent Oil: Brent oil is a basket of oil consisting of crude oil extracted from four wells of British and Norwegian oil in the North Sea. Brent oil is one of the most important sources for pricing other oils in the world.

WTI (West Texas intermediate Oil): WTI is US oil extracted from West Texas. It is a light oil and is used as a very important pricing criterion for the rest of the world.

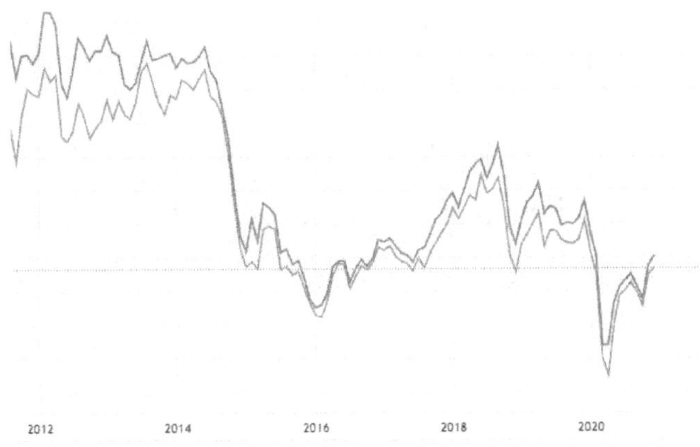

In the chart above, the red line is the Brent oil price trend and the blue line is the US oil trend. We see the strong dependence of these two oils on each other, and we also see that Brent oil is generally more expensive than American oil.

OPEC: OPEC is an oil basket produced by OPEC member countries. There are now 13 OPEC members. Algeria, Angola, Congo, Guinea, Gabon, Iran, Iraq, Kuwait, Libya, Nigeria, Saudi Arabia, UAE, and Venezuela are the 13 members of OPEC.

The OPEC basket is a combination of different heavy and light oils of countries. The heavy oil in the OPEC basket is heavier than Brent and West Texas   Intermediate.

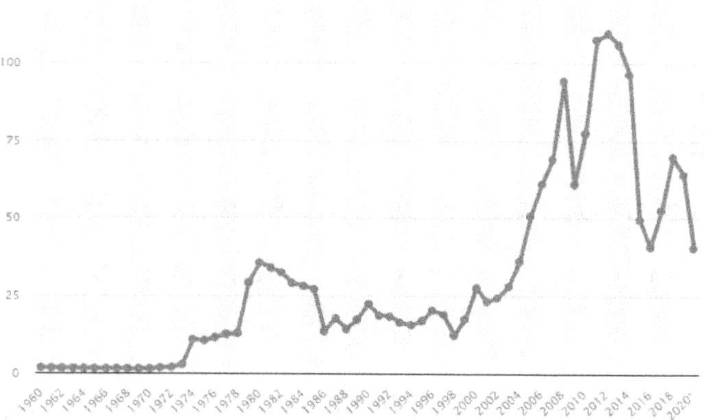

In the chart above, we see the OPEC oil trend from 1960 to 2020. Iran's oil is in this basket and the price of OPEC oil is really important for us. As we see, OPEC oil is over 100 dollars from 2010 to 2013. But it fell sharply in 2015 and reached 50 dollars. As a result, the price of oil was almost halved.

Gold

Gold is the most valuable metal in the world. Gold is always used as the safest strategic reserve in risky and inflationary conditions.

An ounce of a gold

Ounce is a unit of measurement used for precious objects. Each ounce of gold traded in world markets is equal to 31.1 grams of 24carat gold. This means gold with a purity of 99.99%.

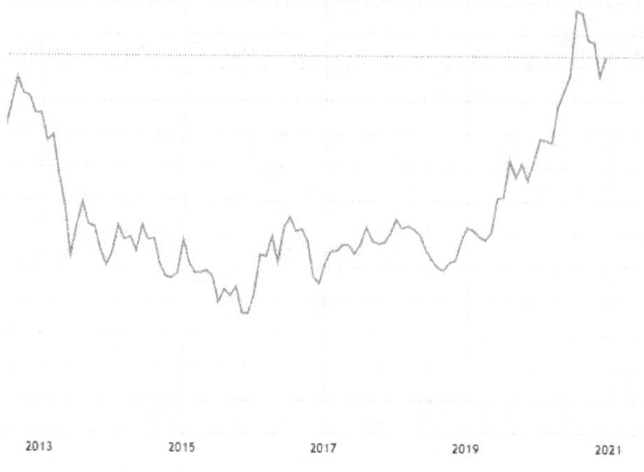

We see the Ounce of gold chart. As we see, the chart has been rising since 2019. Gold always rises when the economy is at risk. For example, since 2019, the US-China trade war and corona virus have pushed up gold prices.

Tax

Taxes are one of the main sources of government revenue.

Individuals and companies must pay part of their income and profits to the government for the use of social services and facilities.

There are 2 types of taxes in Iran: direct and indirect taxes.

Direct tax: it is a tax levied directly on real and legal people. The payer is a specific character, Such as payroll tax, job tax, inheritance tax, etc.

Non-direct tax: it is a tax that levied on goods and commodities. Such as import tax or consumption tax.

Currently, in Iran, the corporation's tax rate is 25%. Although it is lower for corporations whose shares are traded on the capital market.

Tax rate(percentage)	country
34	Brazil
30	Australia
25	China
22	Turkey
21	US
18	Switzerland
0	Emirate

In the table above, we see the tax rates of several countries. As we see the tax rate is zero in Emirates.

Exchange

Exchange is an accepted type of money that includes coins and paper. Exchanges are issued by governments.

Each country has its own exchange. For example, the exchange of Iran is rial or the exchange of China is yuan and the exchange of US is the dollar. In another definition, exchange can be defined as foreign money.

Exchange rate

Exchange rate is the rate at which you must spend your national money to obtain the national money of another country. For example, when you say that the dollar rate is 260,000 rials, it means that to get one dollar of foreign country's national money and you have to spend 260,000 rials of your national money.

exchange rate(toman)	year
3017	2012

3338	2013
3425	2014
3757	2015
4899	2016
12894	2017
14903	2018

In the table above, we see the dollar rate on the last trading day of March each year. The growing trend of the dollar has started since 2017.

At some points in 2019, the dollar has reached over 30,000 tomans and was traded at this price.

Reasons for rising exchange rates in countries

Well, you may be wondering why the exchange rate has risen in recent years. One of the main reasons for the increase in the exchange rate is rising inflation. Inflation means the devaluation of the country's national money.

This will automatically increase the exchange rate. Another reason is the issue of supply and demand for currency in the economy. When governments fail to create input sources for the exchange, there is a shortage of exchange in the country, which causes the exchange rate to rise.

Another issue is the government debt. When government debt increases, they may generally print money without backing, which causes inflation as well as an increase in the exchange rate. One of the most important points for choosing a good country for immigration and investment is to discuss the exchange rate of that country with the US   dollar.
A country whose national currency is high against the US dollar is suitable for immigration. In such cases, you must compare the inflation rate of that country with the US. If it was higher, it means that the country does not have a strong currency against the US dollar.

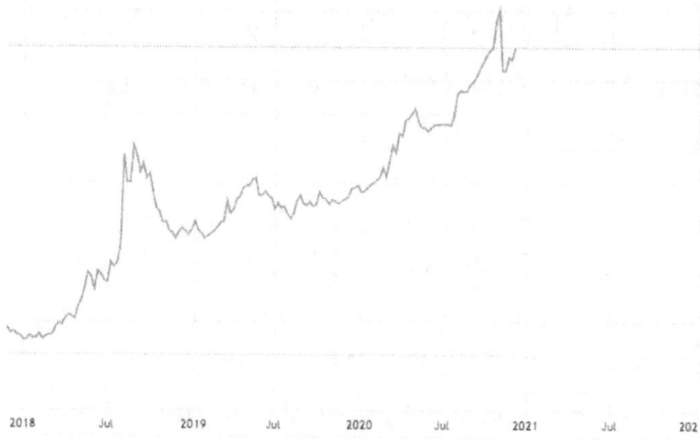

The chart above measures the value of the US dollar against the Turkish lira. As we can see, from 2018 onwards, the value of the dollar against the lira has increased. That is, the lira has depreciated against the dollar.

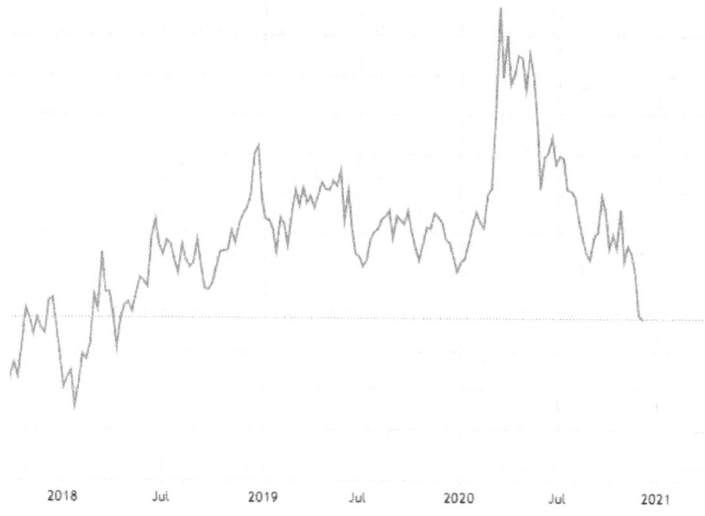

The chart above measures the value of the US dollar against the Canadian dollar. The US dollar has become more valuable since 2018, and this will continue until almost mid-2020. But then, the chart is declining. This time, it's the Canadian dollar that has risen against the US dollar.

Financial markets Market is a place where buyers and sellers interact. The modern form of human life has taken the market out of a certain geographical location.

Financial markets are the markets in which financial assets are traded, such as stock or debt securities.

In the stock market, the company's stocks are traded. Stock means your ownership of the company and you own that company as much as your stocks.

In the debt securities market, debt _like instruments are traded such as corporate bonds or treasury bills. Corporate bonds are papers that represent the participation of their holders in a project. Suppose that an automotive company requires additional capital to launch a new production line. The company issues corporate bonds and provides the required financial resources by selling them to investors.

Each investor will contribute to the partnership in proportion to their capital. In addition, the project must have an economic justification for the issuance of corporate bonds. If this project is approved by the Central bank or securities and exchange organization (SEO), the company will obtain a license to issue corporate bonds and the interest paid will also be determined according to this justification plan.

The publisher company pays a specified and guaranteed interest to the investors at regular intervals as an interest on account. It should be noted that the interest of corporate bonds is guaranteed by banks or reputable financial and credit institutions. After the end of the project, the company calculates the final interest. If the final interest of the project exceeds the interest on account, the difference will be paid to the investors. But if the company has lost, the guarantor is responsible for compensating the difference. Treasury bills are also the papers that the government issues to cover its budget deficit as well as to pay its creditors. No interim interest is accrued on treasury bills and your only profit is the difference between the purchase price and the face value. For example, if today you buy each treasury bill for 82000tomans, the government guarantees that it will buy them from you at a face value of 100,000tomans at a specified maturity. These securities have a maturity of less than a year and are almost risk _ free. Because you exactly know that you'll receive a certain amount on the maturity date.

اسنادخزانه-م3بودجه99-011110 (اخزا903) - بازار ابزارهای نوین مالی فرابورس

خرید	معامله		فروش	بازه روز	672,312	663,011
671,498	672,312 4,973 [0.75%]		682,000	قیمت مجاز	700,705	633,973
اولین	پایانی		دیروز	بازه هفته	680,000	662,376
664,099	**670,780** 3,441 [0.52%]		667,339	بازه سال	682,630	628,058

تعداد معاملات	69	تعداد سهام	50 M
حجم معاملات	189,540	حجم مبنا	1
ارزش معاملات	127.14 B	سهام شناور	%
ارزش بازار	33,539 B	میانگین حجم ماه	123,507

| أخرین اطلاعات قیمت: | 12:29:32 | EPS: | P/E: | P/Eگروه: |
| وضعیت | مجاز | | | |

Above, you can see an example of treasury bills which is used to cover the budget deficit in2019. Its last transaction was in the range of 67000tomans and the maturity date is also highlighted. This means that if you buy treasury bills now and keep them until maturity, you will be given 100,000tomans for each paper on the maturity, which is the face value.

Exchange market

as mentioned, the exchange market represents the stock market. Stock is a risky asset and its value may change.

We measure the exchange market trend with the total index of the exchange market. In fact, the total index of the exchange market is the market thermometer.

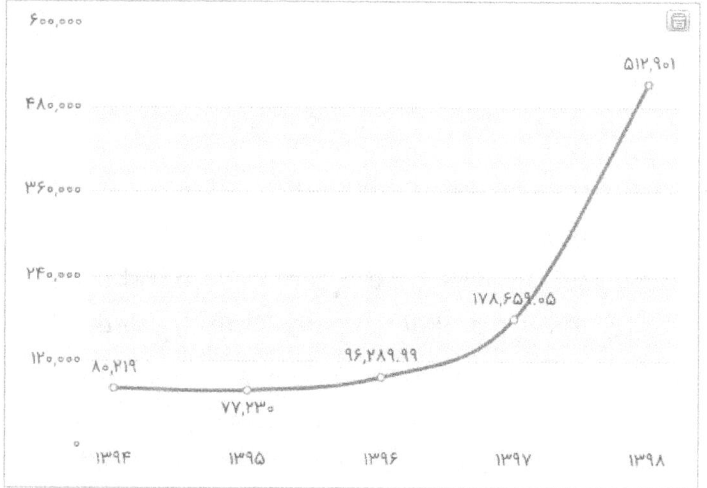

The chart above shows the exchange index trend in Iran. As we see, the exchange market has experienced a good growth since 2017.

The main reason could be that Iran has had a high inflation rate since 2017 and the exchange rate also jumped significantly. In the summer of 2019, the exchange market index reached over 2 million units. This means 300% growth compared to the end of 2018. This growth was mostly because of the entry of people's liquidity into the market.

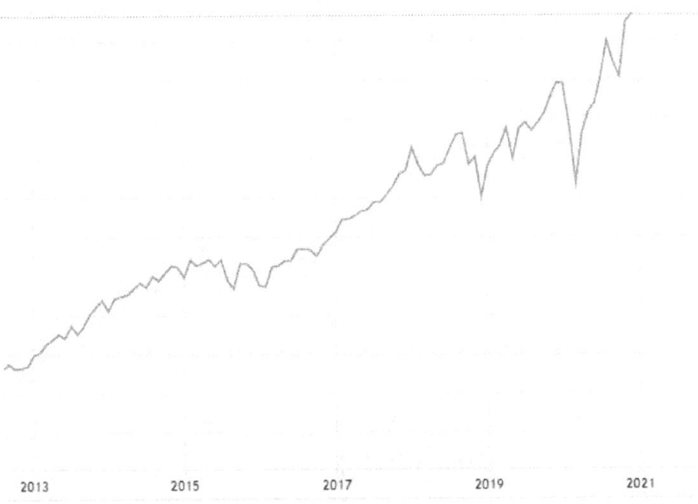

We see the US exchange index which has been growing since 2013. IN the early 2020s, it experienced a major setback due to the spread of corona virus. But after that, it was able to return to its growth. Generally, the exchange market shows strong negative and often short _term reactions to risky events such as the September 11th event.

Budget

Budget is an estimation of revenues and expenses. In fact, in the budget, the strategies for earning money as well as the items of expenses are specified. Besides, the budget represents the goals and the ways to achieve them.

In this section we want to discuss the government budget.
In Iran, the source of government revenue is either from the sale of oil or through the sale of capital assets, such as stock or tax.

The expenses are also divided into two categories: current and construction expenses.

As mentioned, the government can have a budget deficit or a budget surplus. Whenever the revenues are less than the expenses, we have a budget deficit and whenever the revenues are more than expenses, we have a budget surplus.

The government' heavy budget deficits cause more inflation in the economy. To determine this issue, the ratio of budget deficit to GDP can be used. The higher this ratio, the more budget deficit we have compared to GDP, which is likely to cause inflation.

The chart above is the ratio of budget deficit to GDP .Its growing trend has started since 2012 and this ratio is increasing more and more numerically.

This ratio has also increased in US. Since 2015, the US government has faced a larger budget deficit than its GDP.

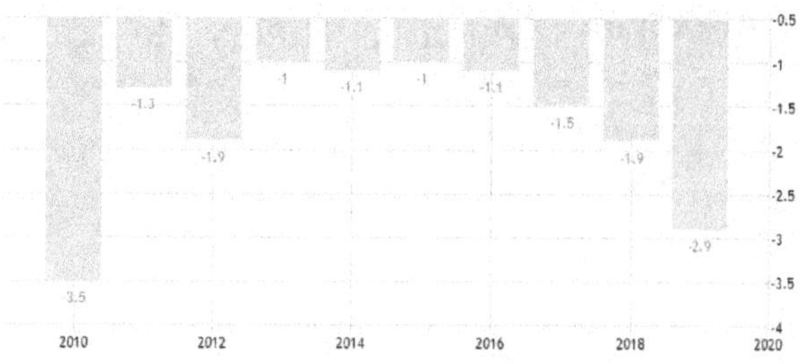

You can see this ratio for Turkey as well.